GW00788958

BEYOND THE EMPTY QUARTER

Beyond the Empty Quarter

TIM OWEN

SERENDIPITY

First published in 2003 by
Serendipity
Suite 530
37 Store Street
Bloomsbury
London

British Library Cataloguing-in-Publication data
A catalogue record for this book is available from the British Library

ISBN 1-84394-067-1

Printed and bound in Europe by the Alden Group, Oxford

Dedication

HM Sultan Qaboos bin Said al Said
and the Omanis

Contents

Foreword

My memories of Tim Owen stretch back half a century to the time we both studied Arabic in the Lebanon, meeting up later on numerous occasions in various parts of the Middle East. Those occasions were a laugh a minute; but this did not conceal Tim's deep understanding of the Arab World and appreciation of the Arabs themselves. As for the Arabs, be they heads of state, rich businessmen, desert tribesmen, or ordinary people, they found themselves in sympathetic touch with a breed of Englishman about whom their fathers and grandfathers had perhaps told them when they were infants and for whom they had inherited a natural inbred respect and admiration.

This book gives a rich account of just a few of Tim's experiences in the Arab World. Occasionally the British Establishment comes in for a mild knocking, something which would not trouble Tim too much; but for the Arabist it is a reminder that good Anglo-Arab relations were built upon the close ties built up over many years by individuals like Tim Owen who lived amongst them and earned respect, not just for himself but for his country.

Those who know the Arab World will enjoy Tim's account. Others who think that Anglo-Arab relations are manufactured in the Foreign Office will find in it evidence for suspecting otherwise.

Arthur Marshall
CBE
British Ambassador in Aden, 1986–89

First Sighting of the Sultanate

My first sighting of the Sultanate of Oman was from the deck of the cruiser HMS *Ceylon* in the autumn of 1957 as we proceeded up the Gulf of Oman and through the Strait of Hormuz en route to Bahrain. A line of rugged mountains was all that was visible to the naked eye.

At the time I was serving in the Royal Marines as Intelligence Staff Officer to the hundredth and last Commander-in-Chief of the East Indies Station, Vice-Admiral Hilary Worthington Biggs, known to his wife, and everybody else for that matter, as 'Blogs'. In Bahrain the Flag was transferred to another cruiser, HMS *Gambia*, which involved packing all one's goods and chattels and moving to another ship. After visiting Kuwait, Basra in Iraq, and Abadan in Iran, on our way back from the Gulf we called in at Muscat, capital of the Sultanate of Oman. Our arrival in Muscat Bay was most impressive. Being an official visit, it required a National salute of 21 guns, which was fired from a saluting gun on the deck of HMS *Gambia*. The thunder of the gun reverberated off the cliffs surrounding the bay on which were inscribed in white paint the names of British warships and others which had visited Muscat over the preceding decades. The local rainfall was so small that it was insufficient to wash off the paint. These names were referred to by the Sultan, Said bin Taimur, as his visitor's book. The return salute fired from cannons on the ramparts of Fort Merani, overlooking Muscat, was even more impressive. After each cannon was fired a majestic black smoke ring rose into the sky before slowly dissipating. The cannon bore the arms of King George III, who presented them to the Sultan of Oman.

Arising out of this official visit by the Commander-in-Chief of the East Indies Station was some correspondence between the British Consul-General in Muscat and the Foreign Office in London on the subject of a National Anthem of the Sultanate. It was customary for the bandmaster of the C-in-C's Royal Marines band in the flagship to hold scores of all the National Anthems of the countries on the East Indies station. Lacking a copy of the score of the National Anthem of the Sultanate, a signal was sent by the C-in-C to the Consul-General asking for a copy for his visit to Muscat, but received a reply that no such score was available. The matter was taken up by the Admiralty with the Foreign Office, who asked the Consul-General for an explanation. In his reply now made famous, the Consul-General explained that he had investigated whether a B flat clarinet score enclosed with the Foreign Office despatch was a correct and up-to-date rendering of the National Salute to the Sultan of Muscat and Oman. He went on to say that the Manager of the British Bank of the Middle East could read music but unfortunately did not have a clarinet. However, he had discovered that the bandmaster of a cruiser in 1932 had composed a 'Salutation and March to His Highness the Sultan of Muscat and Oman'. He was forwarding a recording of this on one side of a gramophone record. A long-time resident of Muscat said it reminded him of a tune once played by the long defunct band of the Muscat infantry, the words of which according to the British military vernacular were: 'Gawd, strike the Sultan blind'. The last occasion it was known to have been played was at a reception given by the Military Secretary in honour of the Sultan, who inadvertently sat on the record afterwards and broke it.

My first and only sortie ashore on this occasion was short and sweet. I had landed from one of Gambia's boats at the town jetty below Fort Merani, which dries out at low tide, and had only proceeded a short distance armed with a camera when a jeep drew up beside me and the driver, a European, invited me to come back for tea. Now, I have never been known to refuse a free meal, or a free drink for that matter, so I jumped in beside him and we proceeded a short distance to his flat inside the walls of Muscat. After tea he drove me back to the jetty, from where I returned to ship. That was the totality of my first visit to Muscat. Little did I realize at the time how much more I was to see of my host, who turned out to be Colonel Hugh Boustead, or of the Sultanate of Oman.

Colonel Hugh was one of a breed of colourful British characters to be found in the Middle East, who sadly are now extinct. At the time he was Development Secretary to Sultan Said bin Taimur. Some years later while staying with him in Abu Dhabi where he was British Political Agent, I asked him why he had left the post of Development Secretary in Oman. He told me that on a visit to the Sultan in Salalah, the Sultan showed him some carpets he had brought on a recent visit abroad and how much he had paid for them. As this exceeded his annual grant to the Development Department, Colonel Hugh decided it was time to move on.

A slight digression on to the subject of Colonel Sir Hugh Boustead, as he eventually became, is irresistible.

As I write from memory of some of the details of his career which he gave me, some inaccuracies are inevitable. Having joined the Royal Navy shortly before the outbreak of the First World War, he found himself as a sub-lieutenant in a ship swinging round a buoy in Scapa Flow after the start of the War with nothing to do and nowhere to go, as the bulk of the sailors had been given a pair of shore service boots and a rifle and sent over to Belgium to back up the Army which was taking considerable punishment from the Germans. Seeing no future in this, Hugh Boustead deserted from the Royal Navy and joined the Army, emerging at the end of the conflict with considerable distinction and decorations, but with the added embarrassment of being a deserter from the Royal Navy. The problem was solved by the granting of a Royal pardon. After a spell at university Hugh Boustead went on one of the early unsuccessful Everest expeditions before joining the Sudan Defence Force which he rose to command. In the Second World War he disappeared into the fastnesses of Ethiopia with the Sudan Defence Force to dislodge the Italians. This having been successfully achieved he spent his final years in the Sudan with the civil administration until independence in 1956. From the Sudan Colonel Hugh went to Mukallah in the East Aden Protectorate as Administrator before moving on to Oman and subsequently to Abu Dhabi.

Between 1961 and 1965 when I was the Royal Navy's Intelligence Officer for the Persian Gulf region, I used to stay with Colonel Hugh at the British Political Agency in Abu Dhabi, of necessity, as at that time there was nowhere else to stay. Abu Dhabi consisted of the crumbling Ruler's Fort, the British Political Agency compound, a few permanent buildings including a branch of the British Bank of the Middle East and a collection of *barasti* huts, constructed of dried date palm branches. There were no paved roads. Staying with Colonel Hugh was an education in itself. On his appointment as Political Agent he was shown his office in a separate building by his deputy, and never went near it again. All his business was conducted from his sitting room on the first floor of his residence, and he used to sleep on a camp bed on the verandah outside. When staying there a search behind the cushions on the settee in his sitting room would from time to time divulge the odd Foreign Office telegram.

After a daily post-prandial siesta Colonel Hugh would go for a walk, when I would accompany him on my visits. We would set off in his official Land Rover with Colonel Hugh driving and the Union Flag flying on the bonnet. His driver would be in the back. Having driven so far we would get out and walk with the driver following behind in the Land Rover in low gear. When he had walked far enough Colonel Hugh would re-embark in the Land Rover beside the driver, whilst I would climb in the back. On the way back passing locals would wave at the Colonel and receive a friendly thwack across the shoulders with the Colonel's camel stick in return.

On one occasion he announced that we would be having lunch with the cook that day, whom he had brought from Mukallah via Muscat. For some reason that I have never clearly understood there has always been a close relationship between the Wadi Hadhramaut, at the mouth of which Mukallah is situated, and Indonesia. Arab merchants having made their pile in Indonesia used to return to the Wadi Hadhramaut to live in comfortable retirement, bringing Indonesian cuisine with them. Thus the Colonel's cook was an expert in Indonesian cuisine. We squatted on the kitchen floor for an excellent meal followed by a sing-song accompanied by Arab musical instruments, whilst Colonel Hugh had his siesta on the kitchen floor. I have often wondered since then how many of Her Majesty's emissaries abroad entertain their guests to luncheon on the kitchen floor with a sing-song to follow.

On another occasion I arrived to stay with Colonel Hugh at the start of Ramadhan. Ramadhan had not started when I left Bahrain, but had in Qatar which we transited. On arrival in Abu Dhabi I was told that it had not started as the Ruler, Shaikh Shakhbout, had ordained that it was not to start until he got back from a cruise to Das Island. The Ruler had purchased Prince Rainier of Monaco's yacht complete with naked cherubs round the stateroom ceiling, which, after certain difficulties over payment of Suez Canal dues, had eventually arrived in Abu Dhabi. This was its initial cruise with Shaikh Shakhbout embarked. Colonel Hugh decided that protocol demanded that he should be present to greet Shaikh Shakhbout as he disembarked from the yacht. So after dark we set off in his Land Rover for the unlighted wooden jetty which at that time was the only port facility in Abu Dhabi. On our arrival we found that the yacht had beaten us to it and was already secured alongside the jetty, providing the only illumination of the scene. The tide was out so the yacht was well below the level of the jetty, and a gangway with guard-rails was in position at a steep angle from the jetty to the forward end of the yacht. The Ruler's two sons and other members of his retinue were already waiting there to greet Shaikh Shakhbout. His private secretary, with the good old Arabic name of Bill Smith, could be seen wandering round the upper deck armed with a fishing rod, but that was the only sign of activity on board. Getting bored with waiting I wandered along the jetty to the after end of the yacht where a gangplank with no guard-rails had been positioned from the jetty to the stern of the yacht. In the darkness I could dimly discern a figure on all fours crawling up the gangplank. With a flash of inspiration I rushed back to Colonel Hugh and said – I think Shakhbout is disembarking at the after end. This precipitated a rush to the after end just in time to see Shakhbout step on to the jetty. What provoked him to come ashore that way I do not know. However that was just Shakhbout's way of doing things.

An episode described by Bill Smith illustrates his employer's attitude towards payment of those who worked for him, which was spasmodic in the extreme. The Police were paid as and when he felt like it. Bill was due to go on three months' holiday, for which he was due to receive his salary in advance according to his contract, which as often as not was ignored. On this occasion he reminded Shaikh Shakhbout that he was due to go on holiday in three days' time. Shaikh Shakhbout appeared to ignore the reminder and went on to other business. Next morning there was a loud bang on the front door of Bill's flat, which when he opened it revealed a rather grubby Arab boy, who handed him an equally grubby pillow case stuffed full of something, and announced that Shakhbout wanted the pillow case back. Bill took the pillow case into his living room and emptied the contents on the floor. It consisted of a pile of one Gulf Rupee notes, each note being worth one shilling and sixpence, which represented his salary for the next three months. He had to count the whole lot up, make them into bundles and take them round to the British Bank of the Middle East to be paid into his account. This was Shaikh Shakhbout's way of pointing out: 'Don't remind me that I owe you three months' salary'.

The last occasion on which I ever saw Colonel Hugh was in London. I was crossing Stag Place on my way to the Ministry of Overseas Development when I bumped into him. I was greeted with: 'Hello, you old bastard! Come and have tea with me in my club'. Following my basic principle about free meals, I duly did, and never saw him again. My first and last encounters were both accompanied with an invitation to tea. After leaving Abu Dhabi he returned to England accompanied by his faithful Arab servant. They both failed their driving tests, so he retired in disgust to Tangier, but was shortly afterwards offered a sinecure job in charge of the Ruler's horses at al 'Ain in Abu Dhabi by Shaikh Zayed who had replaced Shakhbout. He died in hospital in Dubai some years later.

CHAPTER 2

An Admiral
Aground

I had been in Bahrain for nearly a year when in early 1962 I was summoned by my boss, Admiral Fitzroy Talbot, who was Flag Officer Middle East. He told me that he was planning an exploratory visit to the Sultanate of Oman accompanied by his wife, a daughter and his Flag Lieutenant. The Admiral was always uneasy at the prospect of being confronted by Arabs who spoke no English, so I was usually taken along to cope with such situations.

We set off from Bahrain in a Pembroke of the RAF and flew down the Gulf to the RAF station at Sharjah in the Trucial States of Oman, where we were met by the Commander of the Trucial Oman Scouts, and set off in a convoy of Land Rovers across the desert towards the Hajar mountains and the Sultanate. A diversion via the Wadi Ghor had to be made through the mountains as the planned route through the Wadi Jizzi was blocked by an overturned lorry with a load of illegal Pakistani immigrants, some of whom were reported to have smallpox. The route through the mountains was spectacular as we threaded our way along the wadi bed avoiding boulders, which had tumbled down the steep mountain sides. We eventually emerged on the coast towards dusk near the fishing port of Khor Fukhan. A tented camp erected by the Trucial Oman Scouts awaited us for our night's stay. It was a perfect evening in March, and we all bathed in the sea under a full moon off a magnificent sandy beach.

After a evening meal in the open, the young British officer in charge of the camp invited me to accompany him on a call on the Wali of Khor Fukhan. His Land Rover was parked in a line of vehicles in the sand, drawn up in the best British military fashion. Having climbed in, rather to my surprise we shot off backwards, to be followed by a blood-curdling scream which reverberated off the mountains behind. We had run over the Arab driver of an itinerant British doctor who had joined us for the night. He had dossed down in the sand behind the Land Rover. That was as far as we got in our call on the Wali. The doctor was hastily summoned, who administered morphine to the driver. Fortunately it transpired that the only damage he had received, apart from to his nerves, was to the back of a hand which he had put up to protect himself as the Land Rover went over him.

The following morning at breakfast every fly along the coast descended on us, and we were treated to the spectacle of the Admiral's wife eating her breakfast wrapped up in a mosquito net.

We set off again along the coast to the border with the Sultanate at Khatmat Malaha, where we said goodbye to the Trucial Oman Scouts and transferred to the tender care of the Sultan's Armed Forces, and were welcomed by the Commander of SAF, Brigadier Hugh Oldman. We proceeded along the coast to Sohar. Here we stayed the night at the headquarters of the Omani Gendarmerie, a paramilitary regiment responsible for border and coastal patrolling. We were greeted by a redoubtable trio of officers, Reggie Twelvetrees, Carl Seton-Brown and Sandy

Gordon. Carl was an enthusiastic slaughterer of wild duck, and took the Admiral off at dusk to slay some duck at the neighbouring *Khor* or creek. They returned sometime later with nothing to show other than a healthy crop of mosquito bites.

The following morning the whole party set off after breakfast to call on the Wali of Sohar, by whom we were royally entertained. The Admiral's daughter and I showed our appreciation shortly afterwards by being violently sick. I think this was probably due to an excess of halwa, a sweetmeat which is an Omani speciality, made basically from flour and sugar and with the consistency of Turkish delight. I have always retained my partiality for halwa, but without the result experienced at Sohar.

At lunchtime there was a spirited argument between Hugh Oldman and Reggie Twelvetrees over whether we should proceed on our journey along the beach or along a coastal track. A magnificent sandy beach extends along the northern coast of Oman for about 200 kilometres from a point near Muscat to the border with what is now the United Arab Emirates. In those days it was much faster to drive along the beach when the tide was out than along the bumpy coastal track. Hugh Oldman won the argument on grounds of seniority and we duly set off along the beach with the Admiral and Hugh Oldman in the leading Land Rover. All went well until we reached Su'adi Point, where there is an island just off-shore and a tidal creek. Hugh Oldman who was driving with the Admiral embarked drove the leading Land Rover confidently into the creek and stuck firmly in the middle. Now, one of the greatest disasters that the Royal Navy can experience is to have an Admiral aground. An emissary was despatched with all speed to the neighbouring village for help which arrived with commendable swiftness in the form of a team of villagers equipped with a rope which they proceeded to coil up on the ground and squat on. A yell from Hugh Oldman to tell them to get a move on received the terse reply: 'Four hundred rupees!' A purple-faced Hugh Oldman responded with a threat to have them all locked up by nightfall in Fort Jalali, the Sultan's prison in Muscat, commonly referred to as the Sultan's guesthouse, if they did not get cracking. This had the desired result and the Commander of the Sultan's Armed Forces with the Flag Officer Middle East were somewhat unceremoniously dragged back on to dry land. The villagers were suitably rewarded for their assistance the following day.

The rest of the journey was completed without incident. At dusk, having reached the end of the beach near Azaiba, the base of the oil company, where a brief stop was made so that the Admiral's wife could meet a former boyfriend in the oil company, we joined the road into Muscat where we reached our destination which was the British Consulate-General situated on the waterfront within the walls and below Fort Jalali on a lofty crag overlooking the Consulate-General.

The Consulate-General, which became an Embassy in 1970, was a fine building, skilfully constructed where it caught the afternoon sea breezes, blowing in from the Gulf of Oman between the isolated crag surmounted by Fort Jalali and the adjacent hills. There was a tall flagpole in the courtyard in front of the main entrance, where formerly by agreement between the Sultan and the British Government, a slave could, by clasping his arms round the flagpole, claim his freedom, and was issued with a manumission certificate by the British Consul. I was horrified some years later when calling on the Ambassador and noticing that the flagpole had disappeared, to be told that it had been removed to make more room for car parking. The building has recently been vacated and the British Embassy is now in a handsome new building outside Muscat.

We stayed two nights at the Consulate-General and on the day after our arrival the Consul-General, John Phillips, took the party on a boating trip to a neighbouring bay for some scuba diving. I was issued with the usual clobber that one dons on these occasions and given a harpoon gun with which to slay the fish. Setting off I sighted a mottled bulbous fish resting in the water and minding its own business, to which I gave a miss as being too easy a target. My next encounter was with a moray eel, to the gaping jaws of which I gave a wide berth for entirely different reasons. After that I saw nothing other than brilliantly coloured fish, none of which were more than two inches long. On my return I encountered the bulbous fish again, and desperate not to emerge empty-handed, to my eternal shame I shot it through the middle. Triumphantly I stepped out of the water with my catch to be surrounded by an admiring crowd, until John Phillips looked over my shoulder and said: 'I shot that fish half an hour ago, and put it back in the sea.' Shamefacedly I extracted the harpoon and put the fish back in the water, where it lay on its side for a short time, before suddenly righting itself, and swimming off presumably to present itself as a suitable target for the next boating party.

The next day we left the Consulate-General for the airfield at Bait al Falaj outside Muscat where we embarked in an aircraft of the Sultan's Air Force, piloted by a rather disgruntled British Commander of the Air Force. Landing at Firq we did a tour of the fort at Nizwa, the first of many in my case. We then went on to Ibri, where we left the Admiral's daughter and the Flag Lieutenant, both of whom were suffering from air sickness, before flying on to Buraimi where the door fell off as we made a bumpy landing, and the Admiral's wife who was sitting next to the door was nearly jettisoned. Returning, we picked up the Admiral's daughter and Flag Lieutenant, who having been suitably entertained by the Sultan's Army at Ibri, had recovered from their air sickness. The rest of the trip by air back to Bahrain passed without further incident, which completed my first comprehensive tour of northern Oman.

CHAPTER 3

Foiling Arab Smugglers

A rebellion in northern Oman had been quashed by the end of the 1950s, but remnants of the rebels still continued to operate from the fastnesses of the nigh impregnable Jebel Akhdar plateau, laying mines and springing the occasional ambush to the detriment of the oil company's operations. Arms and supplies were being smuggled by dhow from Saudi Arabia and landed at night across the Batinah coast and thence into the interior.

It was one of the duties of the Royal Navy in Bahrain to provide patrols off the Batinah coast to intercept arms smuggling dhows. In the early 1960s frigates were used for this purpose and latterly these were replaced by minesweepers. The situation was apt to be confused by gold smuggling dhows operating out of Dubai to the Indian sub-continent. However the Commanding Officers of the frigates which had a maximum speed of 24 knots soon learnt that if they were outdistanced by a dhow they were chasing, doing 25 knots, that it was a gold smuggler equipped with a powerful diesel engine for avoiding the attentions of Indian and Pakistani customs vessels.

After I had been in Bahrain for 18 months I was due for home leave, but before setting off I had to brief a four-ring Captain of a frigate for a Batinah Coast patrol. He was clearly unenthusiastic about his task, no doubt deeming it rather infra dig for an officer of his seniority.

Not long after I had been at home I received a summons to see the Director of Naval Intelligence at the Admiralty in London. Duly presenting myself at the appointed time on the appointed date I was ushered into the presence of the Admiral, who was seated at his desk with a signal in front of him, which he read out to me. Apparently the aforesaid Captain patrolling at night off the Batinah Coast had made a major arms capture. The frigates used to darken ship when patrolling at night and used their radar to pick up unlighted dhows. In this case they detected an unlighted dhow close inshore, illuminated it with a searchlight and sent a boarding party across. Arms were being jettisoned over the side of the dhow as the boarding party arrived; but a major consignment of weapons, ammunition, radios and other supplies was seized as well as a number of rebel reinforcements. These were duly handed over to the Sultan's Armed Forces. I understand that the Captain of the Frigate was rewarded with the gift of a silver coffee pot by the Sultan.

On my return from leave I despatched Dick Candlish, an Arabic speaking former officer of the Grenadier Guards, who worked with me as a civilian intelligence officer, by air to Muscat with instructions to tell all and sundry in strictest confidence that the interception of the arms shipment was no coincidence, but that we had penetrated the organization to its source and were well aware of details of their activities. This was the most effective and quickest method of spreading information in that part of the world. It worked a fair treat and information came back to us through the normal channels that the message had got back to where it was intended, and the arms smuggling came to a grinding halt.

I had to wait another twenty years to get a silver coffee pot.

CHAPTER 4

Civilianization

After being in Bahrain for nigh on four years, at the beginning of 1965 I started getting concerned over a relief and my approaching retirement from the Royal Marines. I had a feeling that my existence had been overlooked by those responsible in London; so I wrote a letter to the Military Secretary reminding him of my existence. I received a friendly and informative reply. Apparently a problem had arisen over finding a relief for me. My appointment according to Service regulations had to be filled by a Royal Marines officer of Major's rank with an Arabic language qualification, and I was the only one in the Royal Marines. Two officers in turn had been sent to study Arabic at the Middle East Centre for Arab Studies in Lebanon with a view to providing a relief for me, but each was rejected as being non-absorbent of Arabic. This conundrum was finally solved by pretending that one of them had the necessary qualifications and sending him to relieve me. Unfortunately by the time he arrived I had overshot my retirement date, and for administrative reasons I could only retire on my birthday or at the half-year; so on my way home I dropped off in Beirut for an Arabic revision course at MECAS and then spent the remainder of the six month period on indefinite leave.

Whilst all this was in progress, my thoughts became concentrated on employment in civilian life. This was no simple prospect at that time for a forty-five year old.

However, fortuitously, fate played a helping hand. At that time minesweepers of the Royal Navy based in Bahrain had taken over the rôle of anti-arms smuggling patrols off the Batinah Coast of Oman from the Frigates. This made economic sense. However, there was a snag as the minesweepers only had a very limited capacity of fresh water, so that after only a few days on patrol they had to return to Bahrain to top up with fresh water. This was a serious limitation. I was summoned by my boss, the Senior Naval Officer Persian Gulf, Captain 'Splash' Carver, and told to fly down to Muscat and use my initiative in organizing a method of replenishing minesweepers with fresh water at Muscat. So I duly took off for Muscat with a portable pump, and on arrival used my contacts in the Sultan's Armed Forces to borrow a length of hose. I then arranged to hire a water bowser from Khimji Ramdas, a local merchant, who had the only two civilian water bowsers in Oman at that time. When all was ready the minesweeper on patrol came into Muscat Bay and moored as close as possible to the town jetty, from where the hose was run out to the minesweeper and connected to the portable pump on the jetty, which in turn was connected to Khimji Ramdas' s water bowser. The whole thing worked a fair treat, but unfortunately the bowser did not hold enough water to complete the replenishment of the minesweeper's tanks. So it had to be sent off to a water well at a small village outside Muscat called Ruwi to refill with fresh water.

Meanwhile, with nothing to do, I wandered off along the jetty until I came to a building with a brass plate outside the entrance with 'Petroleum Development (Oman) Ltd' inscribed on it. I wandered in dressed in uniform, and seeing an office door ajar, I went in. A European sitting behind a desk looked mildly surprised at seeing this figure in uniform coming in unannounced and uninvited. It turned out that it was Dick Clough, the General Manager of the Oil Company, whom I was confronting. Ignorant of this fact, I announced baldly that I was looking for a job. He took it remarkably well; and after a brief discussion on who I was and what I was doing, he said he would be coming through Bahrain in a few days' time and would contact me. With that I left and went back to the jetty, by which time the water bowser had returned and the operation of replenishing the minesweeper with fresh water was satisfactorily completed. I flew back to Bahrain, and a few days later Dick Clough was as good as his word and contacted me as he was passing through Bahrain on his way back to London.

Rather over six months later I was back home, living at Deal in Kent, by now out of the Service, and on the dole, when I received a telephone call from Shell Centre asking me if I was still looking for a job. I was invited to come up to London for an interview at Shell Centre. On arrival I was ushered in to see a youngish man, who in the course of the interview told me that he had only recently returned somewhat precipitately from Oman, where he had been head of the Management Liaison Branch in the Oil Company. He had apparently made critical remarks at a private dinner party at which only Europeans were present about the way the country was run. His criticisms were reported back to the Sultan in Salalah and he was given a fortnight in which to get out of the country. Two points I remember particularly about this interview. I asked what salary I would get if employed in Oman and was told it would be £5,000 a year plus allowances, tax free, which would be enough to keep me in caviar and smoked salmon. Having been told that my job would be in the interior of Oman and knowing a fair amount about the conditions there, I asked what accommodation I would get. I was told that, as senior staff, I would get an air-conditioned caravan.

I returned home and was shortly afterwards contacted again by Shell Centre, who told me that if I was prepared to take the job I should be ready to fly out to Oman at the beginning of December. Looking back on it, if I had not been sent down from Bahrain to Muscat to organize the replenishment of a minesweeper with fresh water, and wandered into the office of the General Manager of PD(O) Ltd, I would never have got a well paid job in Oman. I always feel I owe a debt of gratitude to Dick Clough for the part he played in this. It is curious how fate plays a hand in life.

CHAPTER 5

Introduction to the Interior

It was with some apprehension that I set off for Oman in December 1965. My journey by air took me via Bahrain and Doha in Qatar to PD(O)'s airstrip next to Azaiba camp, where I arrived at sunset one evening. I had already decided to volunteer to go immediately into the Interior so that my predecessor could show me round and introduce me to those with whom I would be dealing. However, on arrival I was met by him and informed that he would be leaving by the 7.30 a.m. flight from the civil airport at Bait al Falaj the next morning and that I would be required to drive him there. My briefing therefore was limited to a chat over a drink that evening, and next morning I duly drove him to the civil airport early and saw him off.

On returning to Azaila I found that the post of head of my branch was still vacant following the hasty departure of the previous one, who had interviewed me at Shell Centre in London. Acting in his place was Melvin Watterson, well versed in local affairs and of considerable assistance in helping me through my initial stumbling paces. My own team consisted of a clerk Salim bin Said al Siyabi, three drivers, two of whom were Bedu and one Baluchi ex-SAF, and a Baluchi cook.

Although Salim was classified as a clerk he was a great deal more so far as I was concerned, being a guide and mentor without whom I could not have managed. He had left Oman and joined the Bahrain State Police, where he rose to the rank of sergeant-major. On learning that oil had been discovered in Oman in commercial quantities he wisely returned and joined the oil company. Advancement in the oil company was strictly limited for Omanis at that time as Sultan Said bin Taimur stipulated that only Europeans could fill the posts of senior staff Omanis were limited to intermediate staff positions. After the succession of Sultan Qaboos bin Said in 1970 Salim progressed rapidly. Leaving the oil company for the new Ministry of Information, he rose to be Director-General of Radio and Television and then Head of Administration. His career was abruptly terminated at an early age following a major heart attack during Ramadhan after taking violent exercise to get his weight down when fasting. I lost a very good and loyal friend with his death.

Salim spoke fluent English, but was given to expressing himself in a clearly defined manner on occasion. I remember once calling on Shaikh Ahmed bin Mohamed al Harthi at Qabil, who was the premier Shaikh of the Sharqiya region, a sort of viceroy of the Sultan. He was clearly annoyed with me for having taken some action on behalf of the Oil Company which did not suit him. Shaikh Ahmed rattled away at Salim in Omani Arabic for about five minutes, not a word of which I understood, following which Salim turned to me and said simply: 'Shaikh Ahmed says that he detests you.'

I spent Christmas of 1965 at Azaiba and left immediately afterwards for the Interior with my team in three Land Rovers. We made our way up the Sumail gap through the mountains along the graded road maintained by the Oil Company. On emerging from the mountains we turned south along another graded road, finally arriving at the site of Party 15, a seismic party. By this time I had lost all idea of where I was, apart from being somewhere in the interior of the Arabian Peninsula. It turned out that the site was on a stretch of level ground alongside the Wadi Halfayn. Our camp was a collection of tents adjacent to the camp of Party 15. When I asked where my air-conditioned caravan was, which had been referred to in my interview at Shell Centre, I was shown a tent and told that that was my tent, and so it remained for the next year. The summers in Oman are very hot and you cannot air-condition a tent. My one contact with modernity was an electric light bulb in my tent supplied with power from Party 15's generator.

On my first night, tired after a busy day, I went to sleep early only to be woken by a feeling that I was not alone in the tent. I switched on the light and saw what I assumed to be a murderous figure leaning over me, but who turned out to be a very agitated tribesman. Somehow I summoned Salim who established that the man was a Janaba tribesman who was living nearby with his family in the bed of the Wadi Halfayn near a water well. His wife was about to give birth but was having problems. Now, I had done many and varied courses in the Royal Marines including first aid, but never midwifery. After a hasty discussion it was decided to put her in one of my Land Rovers and send her to a clinic at Adam about ten miles away up the Wadi Halfayn. So she and her husband and family were put in the back of the Land Rover with their belongings, which bumped its way up the Wadi bed to Adam. I never heard what happened after that; but if the baby did not arrive on the way to Adam it was not my fault.

Being told by Salim that I should make an early call on Shaikh Khamees, the tameema Shaikh of the Janaba tribe, in whose territory we were camped, we set off a few days later down the Wadi Halfayn to find him. This was done by asking each beduin woman we saw where we could find Shaikh Khamees's tree. The division of labour between bedu men and women was quite simple: the men looked after the camels and carried rifles, and the women did everything else. One of the women's tasks was watching over the goats when they were grazing. If a goat wandered too far they hurled a stone at it. Their aim was extremely accurate, and they would have been an asset to any cricket team. I soon learnt to keep out of the line of fire.

We eventually ran Shaikh Khamees to ground at his tree in the bed of the Wadi Halfayn. His home, or fareeg as it was known, consisted of a few mats thrown over the top of a flat-topped thorn tree to give additional shade, some rugs spread on the ground underneath, and a fire. That was about the lot. Courtesy demanded that we should be entertained on arrival; so we squatted in a circle on rugs, whilst coffee was brewed up in a brass coffee pot over a fire consisting of about three sticks, and dried dates on a tin plate were offered round. The art was to brush the flies off with one hand and grab a date with the other before the flies landed again. The bedu lived under trees, which was sensible, as they got the benefit of any breeze that was going, which you did not get in a tent. If it rained, that was the best of good fortune, as it provided good grazing for the animals.

In the course of my conversation with Shaikh Khamees it came out that I was going to a village called Izz, away to the north. I had been told by Party 15 that they would be moving shortly, and I would have to find somewhere else for my camp. I suggested Adam, but was told that the Sultan did not approve as Adam was full of thieves

I forbore to point out that the ruling dynasty had its origins in Adam. Considerably to my dismay Shaikh Khamees announced that he would come with me to Izz. His retainers with their rifles and bundles of personal possessions climbed into the back of the Land Rover, whilst Salim drove; and Shaikh Khamees having paid a fond farewell to his wife and family climbed in the front with me squashed in the middle over the gear lever. We arrived at Izz, which was a settled village with date gardens; but Shaikh Khamees wanted to go on down a wadi bed giving directions with his finger. Finally he stopped at a tree where he got out with his retainers and greeted wife and family number two, who were living under the tree, and I was dismissed. This was my first introduction to family life amongst the bedu.

On our way back into Izz we passed a collection of huts like Indian teepees made out of dried date palm fronds. These belonged to the bedu, who at the time of the harvest in August, come in from the desert and gorge themselves on fresh ripe dates, and dry others in the sun. These were then collected as their winter rations when they moved back into the desert. Few people realize that many of the date gardens are owned by the bedu who employ the local villagers to pollinate the date palms in the spring and pick the dates at the time of the harvest.

When we arrived in the centre of Izz all the male population turned out to meet us, identically dressed in brown dishdashas and cartridge belts and carrying a rifle. They stood in a semicircle; and somewhat nonplussed I asked Salim if I should go round and shake hands with them all. He told me that this was not necessary, when a voice called out in English: 'Good afternoon, Major Owen. How are you?' I was even more nonplussed until I discovered it was my former Omani office sweeper in

Bahrain, Abdullah, who happened to be on home leave. In fact we never went to Izz, as I was directed to a camp site close to an Army camp at Izki, where I teamed up with Hugh Massey, who was the Oil Company representative with those constructing the pipeline through the Sumail gap. Hugh had his air-conditioned caravan whilst I had my tent.

CHAPTER 6

Travel without Roads

When I arrived to work for PD(O) Ltd at the end of 1965 I was already aware of travel conditions in the interior of Oman, where only Land Rovers and Bedford trucks, locally known as taxis, could stand up to the prevailing travel conditions. I had never driven a Land Rover, and was, and still am, totally useless when it comes to things mechanical, for the simple reason that I am not the slightest bit interested in them. Changing an electric light bulb represents my limitations in this respect. I asked on arrival if I could have a brief course in engine maintenance, but this was brushed aside. Although I quickly learnt to drive a Land Rover using four-wheel drive, I was always keenly aware that if the vehicle broke down the only thing I was capable of was lifting the bonnet and seeing if the engine was still there.

My drivers fortunately were quite different. Two were bedu, who graduated direct from driving a camel to driving a Land Rover, and the third was a Baluchi, who had previously served as a driver in the Army. Hamid of the Harsusi tribe had an unfailing method of rectifying an engine breakdown. He would lift the bonnet, pick up a stone, bang everything in sight, lower the bonnet, press the starter and away we went. It was an unfailing method as far as he was concerned: it never worked once for me. I only ever travelled with a single vehicle if I was on a known route where other traffic would be passing. I only once got stranded in a single vehicle between Sur and

Ras al Hadd; but I knew that a party of geologists was somewhere behind and would be following the same route shortly. Particularly in the southern desert, where tracks were soon obliterated, routes used to be marked by 40-gallon oil drums spaced out at intervals. The only trouble was that there were discarded oil drums scattered all over the place.

Parties working in the desert used to send water bowsers daily to the nearest well for water, sometimes a considerable distance away. As long as you followed these tracks, if you had a breakdown you knew that a bowser would be coming along within the next 24 hours. My successor with a colleague returning from a rig in the south took a short cut across the desert and broke down. Under these circumstances the only way you could get out of the sun was to get under the Land Rover. Fortunately for them a visiting professor from Newcastle University, who was studying the Harsusi language, visited their base camp and was told that they were overdue. He contacted the PD(O) base at Azaiba by radio and an air search was sent up which spotted them and they were rescued. On these occasions when an aircraft was heard it was the practice to set a spare tyre on fire, which sent up a column of black smoke, which would be spotted by the aircraft.

When travelling over long distances we often had to stop for the night. My golden rule was always to stop away from inhabited localities and cultivation, where malaria was prevalent. The result was that, although I never took any anti-malarial precautions, I never had malaria. The other basic precaution was never to walk around in sandals after dark, as scorpions come out after dark, and if you tread on one you know all about it. Our rations when travelling always seemed to consist of

Jacob's water biscuits, sardines and tomato puree. It had to be Jacob's water biscuits and I knew of one location where the labour went on strike because they were given biscuits other than Jacob's water biscuits with their rations.

One of my responsibilities was to provide well guards with their pay and rations. Some of these wells, such as at Haima and al Ajaiz, were a long distance away across the desert, and I was never very happy about sending a driver out on his own on these occasions, having been brought up in the armed services not to require your troops to do what you were not prepared to do yourself. However this never seemed to worry the drivers. The only trouble was that the bedu have no sense of time, and in spite of being told to be back by a certain day, would drop off to stay with friends for several days leaving me gnawing my fingernails and wondering whether to call for an air search. They were quite incurable in this respect.

CHAPTER 7

Sojourn in Sur

In the spring of 1966 I was told to accompany a geological team to Sur, and generally look after their interests there should problems arise with the local inhabitants. At that time there was nothing resembling a road connecting Muscat with Sur: all communication was by sea. We however had to make our way there overland. We set off from Muscat in four Land Rovers, three of mine and one belonging to the geological party, as well as a Bedford truck loaded with tents and stores. We followed the Oil Company graded road as far as Sumail, and thence by wadi beds as far as Qabil, from where we followed the edge of the Wahiba sands to Kamil and through the mountains to Sur. It is worth mentioning in passing that now there is a broad highway connecting Muscat with Sur with bus shelters along the route, a motel at Qabil and litter bins at intervals. The journey now takes three hours, whereas in 1966 it took two days.

On arrival we set up camp on the sandy beach. I went to call on the Wali, Shaikh Hamood, who told me that he had formerly served in the Trucial Oman Scouts. He asked me, as a favour, if I could lend him a Land Rover whilst we were at Sur, as his only means of transport between Balad (town) Sur and Mina (port) Sur was on donkey back. I gladly did so. At that time Sur consisted of two distinct entities several miles apart. Balad Sur, where the Wali lived and worked, was inland amongst date gardens. Mina Sur was on the coast on the bay, where the inhabitants lived by fishing and a thriving dhow building industry. The only vehicle in Sur belonged to Khimji Ramdas, the Muscat merchant, who had a house in Sur with a swimming pool in the garden, which we were allowed to use during our stay.

Each day the geological party went off about their business. They went to all the places where they were forbidden to go. At that time some of the tribes were deeply hostile to Europeans in that region, particularly the Bani bu Ali, who fired at any European who had the temerity to penetrate their territory. The leader of the geological party told me that the inhabitants of one valley informed him that they had not seen a European since they did battle with Indian troops commanded by British officers. According to my calculations that would have been about one hundred years earlier.

Sur boasted a so-called hospital under an Indian doctor. I would describe it rather as an up-market clinic. There were also two Shaikhs resident there who invited our party to a meal. They were most generous hosts and very liberal in their attitudes towards life. After the meal was finished they lit up cigars and asked me to declare their loyalty to the Sultan, but request him to keep his army away from Sur, as they were quite capable of maintaining the peace themselves. I assured them that on the next occasion I met the Sultan I would pass their message to him, in the full knowledge that there was no chance of such an occasion arising.

The geologists wanted to do some research in the area of Ras al Hadd, which gave me the opportunity of visiting one of the most remote places in the Sultanate at that time. We followed the so-called Savyid Majid road, named after the half-brother of the Sultan and former Wali of Sur. I think it was quite the worst track I ever followed in the whole of the Sultanate. It consisted of a series of near-vertical slopes requiring four-wheel drive most of the way. The geologists went on with their research, whilst I went to Ras al Hadd, where there was a dilapidated fort and small village, all of whose occupants turned out to greet us. After coffee with the headman, we inspected the main features of Ras al Hadd, which consisted of a magnificent sandy beach and a large hard-surfaced landing strip, constructed by the Americans in World War II as a staging post for their aircraft.

Shortly after leaving Ras al Hadd on our return we broke a half-shaft in the Land Rover whilst driving along a particularly rocky wadi bed. This meant that we could no longer get into four-wheel drive, and so came to a grinding halt at the next steep climb. Fortunately the geologists were behind us and had to return by the same route, so after a two hour wait they caught up with us, and abandoning our Land Rover we climbed into theirs and got back to the camp without further incident.

The abandoned Land Rover of course had to be repaired and rescued, so I called up Azaiba on the radio and explained the problem. It was arranged that a new half-shaft would be flown down to the air-strip at Ras al Hadd, where we would collect it. Rather than face the Sayyid Majid road again, I chartered a dhow and went by sea to Ras al Hadd, where the dhow anchored offshore and I swam ashore, whilst the others rowed ashore in a small boat belonging to the dhow. The aircraft, a Heron, duly arrived and disgorged most of the senior staff from Azaiba who had come for the outing. The new half-shaft was handed over and they flew back to Azaiba. I decided to swim back to the dhow whilst the others with the half-shaft rowed back. Just short of the dhow I was caught by the current and found myself being swept out into the Indian Ocean. Try as hard as I could I was unable to make headway against the current and yelled for help. A line was let out from the dhow which I was able to grab as the current swept it down towards me, and greatly relieved I was hauled back to the dhow. It taught me a sharp lesson. On our return to Sur I sent two of my drivers with the half-shaft to the abandoned Land Rover, and it was brought back safely to the camp.

Just as we were about to leave Sur news reached me of an unsuccessful attempt to assassinate the Sultan in Salalah. Sometime later I was given an account of what happened from someone who got it first hand from the Sultan. At that time in early 1966 the Sultan had his own private army in Salalah called the Dhofar Defence Force, officered by Pakistanis and equipped with scout cars. The Sultan's Armed Forces were not allowed into Dhofar. It had been decided to put the Dhofar Defence Forces through a day of exercises to be witnessed by the Sultan. On completion the Sultan was to be given a royal salute by a guard of honour. Accordingly the Sultan stood on a dais with the guard of honour in front of him. On the appropriate order being given the soldiers brought their rifles up to their shoulders and blazed away at him from fifteen yards range. Bullets whizzed past the Sultan to left and right as well as over his head, and he was untouched. The soldiers stared aghast, decided he was immortal, turned on their heels and fled to join the rebels in the mountains. That was the end of the Dhofar Defence Force.

On our way back from Sur I was driving a Land Rover with Salim bin Said al Siyabi sitting beside me. Normally I never discussed Omani politics with Omanis as a matter of policy. They were very arcane anyway. As there was no one present I asked Salim who would succeed the

Sultan when he left the scene. After some hesitation Salim said: 'Savyid Tariq, I suppose'. Savyid Tariq was a half-brother of the Sultan, who had distinguished himself during the Jebel rebellion in the north and was generally popular. So I said: 'What about the Sultan's son, Savyid Qaboos?' To which Salim replied: 'Nobody has ever seen him'. I describe this incident as it was a prevalent attitude in Oman at the time. When, four years later, Sultan Said bin Taimur was deposed and succeeded by his son, Sultan Qaboos flew from Salalah, where he had been, to all intents and purposes, incarcerated for the last six years, to Muscat, his capital which he had previously never visited, to be seen by his subjects who had never seen him. It was hardly an auspicious start to a reign. Against this background the developments and achievements of the Sultanate of Oman under the leadership of Sultan Qaboos are all the more remarkable, a view strongly supported by all Omanis.

CHAPTER 8

Mugged on the Ibri Road

The Sultan ordained that all unskilled labour required by exploration parties operating on behalf of the Oil Company should be recruited from the tribe of the area in which the exploratory operations were taking place. After the tribal Shaikh had taken his ten per cent cut, the tribesmen, for lack of any alternative banking facilities in the interior, used to bury their savings in a tin under a selected identifiable tree. This practice led to a complication on one occasion in the late 1960s when I was looking out for Rex King, the Company representative in Ibri who was away on home leave. Rex, who became something of a living legend in the Ibri region during his tenure of office, lived in comparative luxury compared with my existence in a tent. He lived in a bungalow with a garden and a swimming pool, adjacent to an Army post on the edge of Ibri. Rex knew how to look after himself He had an excellent Goan cook, and used to scour the countryside for bits and pieces to improve the amenities of the bungalow. His greatest trophy was undoubtedly an undamaged lavatory pedestal, which he found sitting in majestic isolation in the middle of a barren and featureless landscape near Haima in the south.

At that time the currency of the Sultanate, apart from the Maria Theresa dollar which freely circulated, was the

Gulf Rupee, which was identical in all respects with the Indian Rupee apart from the colour of the notes. In those days before they developed their own currencies, the Gulf Rupee was common to all the Gulf States. Whilst I was in Ibri an instruction was issued by the British Bank of the Middle East, at that time the only bank in the Sultanate, recalling all the high denomination notes, which had to reach the Bank in Muscat by a certain date. The tribesmen employed by the parties operating in the Interior immediately demanded transport to take them to their trees to collect the required currency notes. Their request was referred to the Company headquarters on the coast, who turned it down; whereupon they all went on strike. This was where I was called in. I pointed out to the Party Chiefs that as long as the strike lasted they were losing good money: there was a high range of mountains separating them from the HQ on the coast, the occupants of which were not going to bestir themselves from their air-conditioned offices to confirm that their instructions were being carried out and it was logical and financially sound therefore to ignore their instructions and provide the necessary transport. This was seen to be sensible and the transport was duly provided and the strike called off.

I had the task of collecting in all the high denomination notes and getting them to the BBME by the required date. So, on the final day I set off at an early hour in a Land Rover for the long drive into Muscat. There was no road, as such, out of Ibri; only a track connecting it to the graded road between Muscat and the Interior. I had only gone a few miles when I was confronted by a tribesman standing in the middle of the track pointing a rifle at the Land Rover. My first reaction was that it was just my luck to be the first to be mugged for money in Oman. The tribesman came over to the Land Rover and said that Shaikh Ali bin Hilal, the tameema Shaikh of the Duru tribe wished to speak to me. Shaikh Ali was conspicuous by his absence; so I asked where he was. The tribesman indicated a nearby hillock and explained that Shaikh Ali was behind that. So, abandoning all the money in the Land Rover to my driver and the tribesman, I walked round to the back of the hillock, where, sure enough, was Shaikh Ali clutching a large tin, which turned out to contain all his high denomination rupee notes, the fruits of the ten per cent cuts paid to him by Duru tribesmen employed by the various parties operating in the Duru region. It was explained that I was required to take them into Muscat for exchange and return the new currency to him at the same location at a mutually agreed time and date. What was not explained was that it had to be done this way so that none of Shaikh Ali's tribesmen could see how much money he had accumulated. The remainder of the operation went off smoothly. I got the money intact into the BBME on time, and Shaikh Ali got his money back as arranged. As a sweetener the Oil Company built Shaikh Ali a house at Tan'am near Ibri, where the Duru owned the date gardens. After the official presentation Shaikh Ali put the goats into the house, and lived under a tree outside, as he regarded a house unsanitary to live in.

In addition to Shaikh Ali bin Hilal there were two other Duru Shaikhs I had to deal with: Shaikhs Muttah and Hareb. They took it in turn to deal with the Company representative over matters relating to oil operations and affecting the Duru tribe. As far as I can remember they did three-month terms and were known as the Duty Shaikh. They were always demanding the loan of transport to convey their families, goats, and other impedimenta from one location to another. It was

Company policy to accommodate them so far as possible. They had no sense of time, and would return the Land Rover filthy dirty and full of goat droppings several days later than agreed, which used to infuriate me. Shaikh Hareb was the worst offender; so I decided to teach him a lesson. On the next occasion he asked for the loan of a Land Rover on Wednesday, a request to which I readily agreed, which was unusual. I deliberately sent it on Thursday, to be confronted by an indignant Shaikh Hareb a few days later, complaining that I had sent the Land Rover a day late. I explained that as he always returned it a day or more late, I was merely emulating his practice. I had no more trouble with Shaikh Hareb over transport after that.

Shaikh Hareb almost, but not quite, succeeded in getting his own back on me shortly after this. Rex King had returned from leave, and I was about to depart from Ibri when we received an invitation to lunch with Shaikh Hareb. We duly set off for his fareeg which was under a tree in the Wadi Aswad. The meal was in the traditional bedu style. We sat in a circle round a large mat, and a tray was brought in with the meal which had been prepared by the women out at the back. It consisted of a large mound of rice covered with saffron over which were spread pieces of cooked goat meat. On the summit of the mound of rice was the goat's skull complete with eyes, which stared at me reproachfully throughout the meal. It was customary for the host to split open the skull with a knife, gouge out the brains, and hand them literally to the guest of honour for his delectation. On this occasion, however, Shaikh Hareb removed the eyes and handed one to Rex and the other to me. Rex popped the eye into his mouth and swallowed it with great aplomb under the admiring gaze of the others in the circle. Whilst their attention was diverted I buried mine in the mound of rice in front of me. Nothing on earth was going to persuade me to swallow a sheep's eye, far less a goat's eye. I never encountered this again, nor have I ever heard of another European being confronted with this situation in Oman.

CHAPTER 9

Safi –
The Mankiller

I was always fascinated by the position of women in bedu society. They seemed to do all the work with remarkable cheerfulness. They were clothed from head to foot in black and their faces were masked. I would pass them tending the grazing goats, and would often stop to ask directions. They were always most co-operative and forthcoming, and would come over and shake hands, but never physically contact you. A hand would be thrust out under the black garment and you would shake hands through it. When I called on a bedu Shaikh we would sit around in a circle on the ground drinking coffee before getting down to business. Any women who were around would join the circle and join in the conversation, holding their own with the men. This would not have occurred in urban society. They would withdraw when we got down to business.

When invited to a meal with a Shaikh, the women would prepare the meal behind the scenes, but never join the men at the meal. I once remarked that it was rather unfair on the women that they had all the work of preparing the meal, whilst they had to eat the left-overs after the men had finished, but was told not to worry as the women always kept behind the best bits for themselves.

In the 1960s there were no roads other than two of

three graded roads, and the only vehicles that could stand up to the terrain were Land Rovers and Bedford trucks. Much travel in the interior was across country following tracks of oil drums spaced out across the desert to indicate direction. Petrol stations of course were something for the future, so that the Oil Company kept dumps of petrol in 40-gallon drums at water wells where they existed. Land Rovers of course carried reserves of petrol in jerry cans. One of my tasks was to arrange recruitment of well-guards through the Shaikhs of the tribes of the areas where the water wells were situated. The Oil Company used to pay the well-guards and provide them with rations.

The Shaikhs were onto a good thing, as the Sultan stipulated that all recruitment of labour had to be from the tribe of the area and through the tribal Shaikh. It was not unusual when a rig or seismic party moved into a particular area for three different tribes to claim the area. This was where I came in, and endless argument and negotiations would end with a compromise, by which each claimant would take on a third of the jobs. The Shaikhs nominated the individuals, one tenth of whose earnings went to the Shaikh in return for nominating them. There was no alternative employment in the Interior.

On one occasion I had arranged to meet Shaikh Ahmed bin Mohamed al Harthy at a location in Wadi Halfayn where a rig was to move to drill for oil. Shaikh Ahmed had been appointed by the Sultan for overall dealings with the Oil Company in the Sharqiyah region. We duly met and I pointed out on a map where we were in the Wadi Halfayn, to which he replied: 'No, we are not: we are in the Wadi Andam; and anyway I can only read Arabic; so you will have to write all place names in Arabic on the map'. Endless argument and discussion then ensued, ending up with the inevitable compromise. I knew exactly why he insisted that we were in Wadi Andam. The Wadi Halfayn belonged indisputably to the Jenaba tribe, whilst the Wadi Andam belonged to the Wahibah tribe. For his own political reasons Shaikh Ahmed wished to give the recruitment of labour to the Wahibah tribe. By the time I left I reckoned I was highly qualified for a post in the diplomatic service.

At one of the water wells at Afar in the Wadi Halfayn where the Oil Company kept a dump of 40-gallon drums of petrol, there was an unusual situation, as the senior well-guard was a woman called Safi. I never saw anything of Safi except a pair of piercing brown eyes; but that was enough to tell me that here was a very strong character. I visited the Afar well frequently and got to know Safi well. One day I arrived to a scene of great excitement. It was explained to me that a Hollandee (Dutchman) had driven up in a Land Rover and demanded petrol. Safi replied that it was Mr Owen's petrol and that he could not have any. He explained that he also worked for the Oil Company, was entitled to the petrol, and was going to take it: whereupon Safi advanced on him brandishing a baulk of timber, and he hastily got into his Land Rover and drove off – Victory for the female sex.

I reckoned that Safi was in her middle twenties. I once asked Salim, my clerk, if she was married. He replied: 'Good Lord, no!' I asked why not, and Salim replied that the men were far too scared of her to marry her!

CHAPTER 10

Omani Humour and Generosity

Omanis have a great sense of humour with a tendency towards the banana skin variety. They enjoy a good laugh, particularly if you tell a joke against yourself and within reason they do not mind if you pull their legs.

Shortly after I arrived in the Interior in 1965 I had my first taste of Omani humour. Part of my job was to pay the unskilled labour, who were Omani tribesmen. This was a long and drawn out process involving much haggling and argument. One day I was sitting in a tent absorbed in this process when a shadow fell across the table. I looked up and there was a menacing figure hovering over me armed with a halve on the end of which was a small axe blade, but quite big enough to carve a hole in my skull. The figure let a growl of 'ma'ash', meaning 'wages' in Arabic, and this was repeated several times. I would have leapt up and fled the tent if I had not been frozen to the seat with fear. Then I noticed that everybody in the tent was roaring with laughter. It transpired that they had smuggled the local madman into the tent and told him to ask for money to see what effect it would have on me. It took some time for my sense of humour to recover. Incidentally the Omanis are extremely kind to the mentally handicapped, and these days considerable provision is made for them. I later discovered that the Shihu tribesmen of the Musandam Peninsula carried these miniature axes as a badge of office, much in the same way as a city gent carries a rolled umbrella.

A few years ago on a visit to Oman, I went to Sohar in a Ministry car with a driver and another member of the Ministry of Information staff. The driver was a fat and cheerful man. He asked me how many children I had, a question I must have been asked hundreds of times in Oman. It was always a source of fascination to them when I said I was unmarried. I retaliated by asking him how many wives he had. He replied three, one in Seeb and two in Khabourah. I asked him how he divided his time amongst them. The answer was that he alternated between Seeb and Khabourah spending two weeks in each. Now, according to Muslim teaching a man can have four wives at any one time, but must treat them equally. I pointed out that he was not doing so by only spending two weeks in Khabourah with two wives, when it should be four weeks. His reply was that two wives in Khabourah lived in the same house. I riposted that he was married to the wives not the houses, and felt that I had won on points. However, I relate this incident as it was conducted throughout with the utmost hilarity.

After the end of the Jebel Akhdar rebellion in the 1950s a limited amount of rebel activity continued which was merely of nuisance value. This included mine-laying along the roads and tracks. One day I met a bedu family moving back into the Interior from the Batinah Coast. The wife was walking in front with a bundle of firewood on her head, followed by the husband on a donkey and various children on foot as well as a dog. I struck up conversation. I asked the husband if it was not customary for the wife to follow behind the husband, to which he replied without batting an eyelid: 'Ah well, you see, there are still some mines laid along this road'. I suspect another example of Omani humour.

Omanis are notoriously generous with their hospitality, which I have experienced over the years. I first experienced this shortly after I started working in the Interior. I used to travel regularly between Izki where I had my camp, and Qabil to discuss Oil Company matters with Shaikh Ahmed bin Mohamed al Harthi, who was the paramount Shaikh in the Sharqiya region. En route I passed through the town of Muthaibi, where it was customary to call on the Wali, Shaikh Ali bin Zaher al Hinai. On this particular occasion it was during Ramadhan, when all Muslims observe the fast. All my team including a young Englishman were Muslims; so when travelling I found myself observing the fast as well. We had spent the night camped outside Muthaibi and had a meal at first light before going into Muthaibi to call on the Wali. Shaikh Ali was a big man with a loud gruff voice. After the initial greetings he said I must have breakfast. So I replied that I had already had a meal before coming into Muthaibi, and anyway it was Ramadhan; to which he said: 'You are not Muslim, are you?' I said no, I was not. 'In that case', he said, 'you must have breakfast'. To have refused hospitality would have been an insult; so I was sat down on the ground at one corner of his majlis and a meal was put in front of me, including, I well remember, some delicious local honey. Whilst I had the meal the Wali sat in the far corner with the remainder of my team locked in discussion. Though somewhat embarrassing to me, it was a very kind and thoughtful act on the part of the Wali, which I greatly appreciated. This was typical act of Omani hospitality.

I am now in the latter half of my seventies, and am not as agile as I used to be. Once I am down on the ground I have difficulty in getting up again. In recent years Omanis have appreciated that and when I have called on them a chair is produced in the *majlis* for me to sit on. There is one snag about this, which I quickly discovered. A tray with refreshments is brought in and put on the ground in front of me. When I lent forward to pick up something off the tray on the first occasion I nearly landed on my chin in the centre of the tray. Great care has to be exercised by the elderly on these occasions.

CHAPTER II

Settling Labour Disputes

Although there were no trade unions in Oman this did not prevent labour disputes and stoppages, often for the most trivial reasons. Each oil rig and seismic party had a personnel representative, part of whose responsibilities was to sort out such problems. However, usually it did not work out that way. The Oil Company divided its concession area into regions, each one of which had a Management Liaison Representative who acted as the liaison between the Company and the Walis and Shaikhs in his area, and for this purpose had to be an Arabic speaker. In practice on each occasion that there was a major dispute or strike a cry for help would go out over the radio for the Liaison Representative to come and sort out the problem.

I soon learnt that the first thing to do was to go and collect the Shaikh of the tribe involved and drive him to the site of the dispute. I also quickly learnt to ask the Shaikh casually on the way if he was short of anything such as cigarettes or sugar. He would reply that, as it happened, he was clean out of cigarettes. These occasions often involved driving long distances over rough country, as the Shaikh was usually living a considerable distance from the scene of the dispute.

On arrival at the site the Shaikh would go and meet the tribesmen involved. They would squat in a circle with the Shaikh in the middle, and the discussion would get under way. Meanwhile I would go and see the Party Chief, who would anxiously explain his side of the dispute, at the same time pointing out that he was losing so many thousands of pounds a day as long as the stoppage went on. I would then suggest that a couple of cartons of cigarettes for the Shaikh would be the quickest and most effective way of ending the stoppage. I would then be accused of encouraging bribery and corruption, to which I would remind the Party Chief of the amount of money he was losing as long as the stoppage went on. This normally clinched the argument and two cartons of cigarettes would be produced. I would then wander over to where the Shaikh was in consultation with the labour force and ask how things were going. I would be assured that it was a particularly difficult problem and was likely to take some considerable time to sort out, I would then mention that I had put two cartons of cigarettes in the Land Rover as a gesture of goodwill from the Party Chief to the Shaikh, and then wander off again. Two minutes later the consultation would break up, and the Shaikh would come over to tell me that the dispute had been settled and work would resume immediately. After coffee I would drive the Shaikh back to where he was living and return to my camp, the mission having been successfully completed. The same result would be achieved by a bag of sugar placed in the back of the Land Rover.

The secret of success lay in the fact that the tribesmen would do whatever the Shaikh told them to do without question. If he told them to stand on their heads they would stand on their heads. A frequent source of dispute was the absence of Jacob's water biscuits for some reason in the rations as supplied by Spinneys. Jacob's water biscuits were an essential part of the equation.

Another source of dispute was over well-guards. Parties operating in the Interior had to be supplied with fresh water, often from wells a considerable distance away. Tankers would make daily trips from the camps to the wells to fill up with water. By agreement between the Sultan and the Oil Company well-guards were supplied by the tribe of the area, who were paid and supplied with rations by the Oil Company. It was my responsibility to carry this out in my region. If there were no parties operating in the area of the well I would propose that the well should be closed down and the guards paid off. Having received approval for doing so I would go and call on the Shaikh and inform him of what was going to be done and why. This would invariably result in a furious argument, as the Shaikh had the responsibility of nominating each well-guard, and took ten per cent of their wages for doing so. I always got my way in the end, but made myself extremely unpopular in the process.

Language problems were the source of many disputes. Young European employees of contractors spoke no Arabic, and not surprisingly the tribesmen spoke no English. As a result misunderstandings easily arose. Often working in intense heat young Europeans in exasperation would shout at the tribesmen, and this immediately led to trouble. To be shouted at meant a loss of face to a tribesman and a labour stoppage would as likely as not ensue. Work would not resume until the young European was removed, and several lost their jobs in this way.

One of the last jobs I had to do in the field of labour was to recruit Duru tribesmen at Ibri for the start of work on the construction of the pipeline from Fahud, the main oilfield in the Interior, to Mina al Fahal on the coast. For security reasons the pipeline had to be buried six feet underground along the entire route. As usual the task of recruitment was delegated to the Duru Shaikh, who had been told how many men were required. When this was completed the men were put in trucks supplied by the Oil Company and despatched from Ibri to Fahud. The next thing I heard was that they had gone on strike. So I set off from Ibri to Fahud, to find on arrival that when they were told to start digging, they claimed that they had not been recruited to do work like that. Fortunately I managed to persuade them that in fact they had been recruited to do exactly that, and they started work. Otherwise we would have been waiting to this day for the pipeline to be constructed.

CHAPTER 12

Encounters with Wendell

Shortly after I left PD(O) in 1969 and returned to England, considerably to my surprise, I received an invitation from the BBC to appear on the Money Programme, which was to be broadcast live in the evening. On arrival at the White City I was told that I was required to comment on a film to be shown about the war in the south of Oman. All appeared to go off successfully apart from the aftermath. Returning by underground to where I was staying in the late evening I became aware of furtive glances from other occupants of the coach. It was only when I looked in the mirror in my room that I realized the reason for the furtive glances. I still had all my make-up on!

In the longer term my one and only appearance on BBC Television had more beneficial results. I had several requests from various publications to write about Oman. One of these was an invitation from the editor of the *Honolulu Star Bulletin*, published in Hawaii, to write an article on the career of Wendell Phillips, of whom the editor was no admirer. At the time my knowledge of Wendell was limited to the fact that he was a collector of oil concessions in the Middle East. Not for the first time, Bill Peyton, my former boss in PD(O) and an anglicized American, came to my rescue, by providing me with valuable sources of information. The result was a lengthy, if rather sardonic, account of Wendell's career which was despatched to the *Honolulu Star Bulletin*, and was duly published.

Wendell Phillips was by profession a palaeontologist and by trade a merchant adventurer. Having acquired the necessary qualifications in California, he liked to be referred to as Dr Phillips. Following the Second World War his various expeditions in the pursuit of palaeontology led him to the Yemen, where he obtained permission to carry out excavations in the Marib area, the former domain of the Queen of Sheba. Rightly or wrongly the finger of suspicion was directed at Wendell by the Yemeni authorities, who suspected that valuable artifacts were being smuggled out of the country. The result was a sudden and abrupt exit by Wendell from the Yemen. His reappearance in the Dhofar Province of Oman at the invitation of Sultan Said bin Taimur was equally sudden.

Wendell was of insignificant appearance, but with an infinite capacity for acquiring the confidence of those in high places. Officially his presence in Dhofar was as a palaeontologist concerned with the investigation of historic sites in the region. Nevertheless, he emerged from discussions with Sultan Said bin Taimur, who was in permanent residence in Salalah, with an oil concession in Dhofar, which he promptly sold to an American oil company, making himself a millionaire overnight. The fact that the oil company did not find any oil of commercial quality or quantity was not his concern. However, fortified by his success in Oman, he went on to Libya, where he pulled off the same stunt on King Idriss with rather greater success as the oil concessions he acquired proved to be highly profitable. He put his wealth acquired from Middle East oil concessions to good use, by investing it in property in California and Hawaii, with his base in Honolulu. He married late in life and died at an early age in his fifties. A colourful character, his demise was greeted with regret by some and not by others.

Wendell kept a representative in London and a permanent suite in a Park Lane hotel. Not unexpectedly, my article in the *Honolulu Star Bulletin* produced an indignant rebuttal from Wendell, which was published in full in the *Honolulu Star Bulletin*, and in which he demanded to know who was this Major Owen who had been writing about him, though he admitted in conclusion that my article had been well written. I was not surprised therefore when his London representative contacted me with an invitation to have lunch with Wendell in London. On this occasion I think the invitation arose from curiosity as to who I was and was intended to assess me. He seems to have decided that I was some form of British intelligence operator and had been involved in the overthrow of Sultan Said bin Taimur in 1970. As a result I received a further invitation to have lunch with him when he divulged that he was planning to publish a book to reveal exactly what were the circumstances surrounding the overthrow of Said bin Taimur, of whom he was a strong supporter, and who at that time in exile was also a resident of a Park Lane hotel. It was suggested that I might co-operate in the production of such a book. I pointed out that I was not a British intelligence operator and as I was not in Oman in 1970 I could not have been involved in the overthrow of Said bin Taimur. I also added that if I did know anything of the circumstances of the coup and those involved I had no intention of revealing what I knew. The result was that we parted on polite but somewhat frigid terms, and I never met Wendell again. The book was never published.

CHAPTER 13

Retreat from a Palace

In early 1976 I went out to Oman as a freelance writer for the *Economist* and *Middle East Economic Digest*. The war in Dhofar, which had its origins in 1963, had just been brought to a successful conclusion by the Omanis. At that time Sultan Qaboos was living in a house inside the walls of Muscat as the old palace had been demolished to make room for the new official al Alam palace, and the Sultan's new residential palace near Seeb was under construction.

I had managed to obtain an audience with the Sultan at the former Chauncey home in Muscat which was the Sultan's temporary residence. Major Chauncey, formerly of the Indian Civil Service, had been personal adviser to Sultan Said bin Taimur, and had left the country following the abdication of Sultan Said. At the same time I had arranged an interview with the British Ambassador Sir Donald Hawley immediately before my audience with the Sultan, the British Embassy being within walking distance of the Sultan's temporary residence.

At the last moment my audience was switched to the new palace at Seeb, 17 km from Muscat along a single carriageway tarmac road. The British Ambassador had just returned from a visit to Dhofar, where the war had ended a few weeks previously, and was eager to tell me all he had seen and experienced during his visit. I was glancing nervously at my watch as the minutes ticked by, and by the time I left the Embassy I had just 20 minutes in which to get to the palace. The driver drove like Jehu all the way from the Embassy, whilst I sat with my eyes shut for much of the time.

On my arrival at the entrance to the palace grounds the police refused to let the Ministry car in, and I was told that I would have to get out and walk the rest of the way. I followed a winding route through a date garden until I reached the palace, where there was not a living soul in sight. Nonplussed, and not wishing to walk the whole way back to the gate, I walked up the steps to be confronted with a vast door with a gold knob. I turned the knob: the door opened; and a bayonet came out into the pit of my stomach. It was attached to a rifle held by an askar (personal bodyguard) who was seated just inside the door. It is only on occasions like this that my Arabic becomes fluid; and I was told in no uncertain terms to return to the gate, where I found a rather harassed Omani officer aide-de-camp waiting for me to arrive. For the third time I followed the trail to the palace, accompanied by the Omani officer, and this time I got in.

I had been expecting my audience to last 20 minutes, but it went on for an hour. The Sultan, who speaks perfect English, was charming and most informative. He asked me how far I had travelled in Oman, and, as I had hoped and intended, he asked me why I had never been to Dhofar. Every time I had applied to go to Dhofar my application had been blocked, even when it had been approved by his Military Secretary, Brigadier Sir Hugh Oldman, a former Commander of the Sultan's Armed Forces, and before that second in command of the Aden Protectorate Levies, where I had first met him. I explained diplomatically that each time I applied to go to Dhofar there were problems, and he assured me that it was not he who had blocked my applications, and made immediate arrangements for me to be flown to Salalah on my next visit.

A year later when I went out to Oman I was immediately flown to Salalah, and had a most interesting tour of Dhofar. I was flown from Salalah to Rakyut towards the Yemen border. Rakyut was a town of ruins: the only inhabitant was the Naib Wali, on whom I called. The rest of the inhabitants had fled years before. From there I was flown on to Dalkhut, the last coastal village before the Yemen frontier. It too was completely ruined. The local school was in a tent, where I joined a class of young children having a reading and writing lesson. Every time I got an answer right I got a round of applause from the children, which was more than I ever got at my own school.

Those who have ever been in the Armed Services will be familiar with the expression 'Nobody cancelled the last order'. The following year when I arrived at Muscat, I was immediately flown to Salalah again, a process which was about to be repeated in the third year. By this time the revolution had taken place in Iran, and I wanted to visit Goat Island at the top of the Musandam Peninsula, where the Omanis had a small naval base strategically situated at the entrance to the Strait of Hormuz. My request was immediately granted and I was flown up to Goat Island in a Skyvan of the Omani Air Force, which was described by its pilot as a Land Rover with wings. Flying over the Musandam was a great experience. At one moment we were flying a few hundred feet above the ground; the next it had fallen away 5,000 feet below us. When I got back to Muscat there was a message from Salalah: 'Where is Owen? He has not arrived'.

APPENDIX I

Development of
Foreign Relations

I am not attempting to give a detailed description of the development of foreign relations since the accession of HM Sultan Qaboos in 1970. This is done elsewhere, particularly in Ian Skeet's book *Oman: Politics and Development*. I can only describe what I have seen and experienced myself.

When I was living in Oman between 1965 and 1969 there were only two diplomatic representatives resident in Muscat: the Consuls-General of the UK and India. At the time of the accession of HM Sultan Qaboos the Sultanate of Oman was virtually unknown to the western world. This ignorance was in accordance with the policy of his father Sultan Said bin Taimur, who left the conduct of foreign relations to the UK, leading to accusations in the Arab world that Oman was a puppet of the UK. The Sultanate was in a state of war with its southern neighbour, the People's Democratic Republic of Yemen; and its relations with another neighbour, Saudi Arabia, could hardly have been worse at the time of his abdication. It fell to his successor to rectify the situation, and a remarkable achievement this has been over the last quarter of a century. It took five years to bring hostilities in the south to a successful conclusion; and now excellent relations exist between Oman and the united Yemen in spite of internal instability in the Yemen until recently.

Border demarcations have been satisfactorily settled and road communications established Much the same has been achieved with Saudi Arabia. Friendly relations now exist, both countries being fellow members of the Gulf Co-operation Council; and the long desert border has been finally demarcated.

Relations with Iran, another neighbour across the Gulf of Oman, have been skilfully handled. At the time of the revolution in Iran relations were tense over the strategic Strait of Hormuz through which most of the oil of the Gulf is exported. In spite of this, friendly relations with the revolutionary regime in Iran were established and have since been maintained in spite of disputes and strained relations between Iran and other members of the Gulf Co-operation Council.

Following the accession of HM Sultan Qaboos Oman swiftly gained membership of the United Nations, the Arab League and numerous Arab, Islamic and international organizations, and in recent years has acquired a notable reputation in regional and international circles for its role as a mediator in disputes between various states. These achievements have in no way affected the long-standing friendly and close relationship extending over two centuries between Oman and the United Kingdom. In recognition of its role in international relations Oman was elected to membership of the UN Security Council in 1994.

It was the discovery of oil in commercial quantities in 1964 and its exports which started in 1967 which made possible the development of the country over succeeding years. Although every effort has been made and considerable success achieved in diversifying the economy over recent years, the economy will continue to be heavily dependent on the production of oil and natural gas into the foreseeable future. Fortunately the proven reserves of oil have been rising steadily over recent years and the reserves of natural gas have rocketed. The oil industry has now expanded into the world outside Oman, and agreements have been signed with the government of Kazakhstan to help in the development of its oil industry, and in the construction of a pipeline from Kazakhstan to the Russian port of Novorosiisk on the Black Sea coast. Natural gas has for some years supplied the internal requirements of industry, power and desalination plants in Oman; but the discovery of large quantities of natural gas in south central Oman has enabled the construction of a LNG plant in south-eastern Oman, from which exports were planned to start in the year 2000.

Over the last quarter of a century Oman has developed from an isolated and inward looking corner of the Arab world into a well-respected and outward looking member of the international community.

Meeting the Needs of Health

When I arrived to work in Oman in 1965 there was only one hospital in the whole of the Sultanate. This was in Muttrah run by an American mission led by Doctor Thoms and his team of American doctors and nurses, and was fee-paying. Scattered throughout the Interior was a handful of health clinics, one of which at Ibri was run by the Oil Company, PD(O) Ltd.

I was soon to see for myself the lack of medical facilities throughout the Interior during my travels when working for the Oil Company. On the one hand there were epidemics of influenza and measles which periodically swept through the bedouin tribes devastating whole families, news of which never reached the outer world. On the other hand there were the endemic diseases, such as malaria, dysentery, tuberculosis and trachoma which were ever present in the towns and villages. Most visible were the children whose eyes were already affected by the ravages of trachoma and blind people being led around by children. Other sick people were hidden away in mud brick houses, which never saw the light of day. Local treatments such as branding were commonly practised, and it is not surprising that the mortality rate was extremely high, particularly amongst the youngest. Few adults ever reached their sixties.

When my camp was in Izki, I noticed one day that our

locally recruited cookboy was missing. I was told that he was seriously ill at home. I went round to his home to see if I could help; but before doing so I contacted the Muttrah hospital to ask if I could bring him in. I was told that I could do so and to bring his mother with him. His home was a typical mud brick building, windowless and dimly lit inside. He was lying on the ground completely wrapped up in rugs and mats, as was the custom, with his mother sitting beside him. I explained to her that I could bring him in to the hospital at Muttrah, which had agreed to take him, that she could go with him, and that it would cost her nothing. However, she refused, and I withdrew somewhat disappointed that my efforts had apparently been rebuffed. But news travels fast in Oman, and the Wali came round to thank me for my efforts and to explain why my offer had been refused. The incident ended happily as not long afterwards the cookboy reappeared completely hale and hearty. I think it must have been an attack of malaria. This incident illustrates the intense suspicion of modern methods of medicine that existed at the time.

This reminds me of another incident a few years later just before I left the Oil Company. I was asked to accompany the headquarter ship *Relume* of the Middle East Navigational Aid Service to Ras al Hadd, to act as interpreter. An automatic lighthouse was to be set up there, and the exact position was to be plotted in. When we landed from *Relume* we were met by the local headman and most of the inhabitants of the local village. The surveyors having done their stuff an empty 40-gallon oil drum was placed on the exact spot where the light was to be put up. The villagers listened with incredulity whilst I explained to the headman that at the risk of eternal damnation no-one was to move or remove the empty oil drum. They had long ago learnt that the eccentric British did peculiar and unintelligible things, and these just had to be accepted. Before leaving I asked the headman if there was anything that the local inhabitants needed. He replied that there was an urgent need for aspirin; so a message was passed back to *Relume* for aspirin. A boat duly came inshore and a bottle was handed over containing six aspirins. The British were always renowned amongst Omanis for their generosity!

Since the accession of HM Sultan Qaboos bin Said in 1970 I have had the good fortune to visit Oman annually, apart from one year, until 1995, and so have been able to observe development in the country over the intervening years. The advancement in the field of health has been one of the most remarkable achievements. I remember in the 1960s visiting Abu Dhabi, where I stayed in the British Political Agency, and sharing a room with an Omani doctor. He told me that he was the only qualified Omani doctor in existence and had a travelling practice along the Trucial Coast, as he was a voluntary exile from the Sultanate, not approving of the existing regime. It was not surprising therefore that the same doctor, Asim Jamali, was the first Minister of Health under the new regime, a fact I reminded him of when I called on him in Muscat in the early 1970s.

In the early stages of development difficulties were immense. Hospitals and health clinics had to be constructed, and there were no Omani doctors or nurses. All doctors and nurses had to be recruited from abroad. Doctors were Indian or European, and most nurses were Indian. I visited a new hospital in the Interior, where all the nurses were Swedish. By the late 1980s most of the hospital and clinic construction programme had been completed with the advantage that all the buildings were new and the equipment was the most modern. In 1986 the Qaboos University was opened near Muscat, which included a medical faculty and hospital. Meanwhile Omani doctors and specialists were being trained abroad, and by the middle 1990s Omani doctors trained at the University were coming into practice. Omani nurses are now rapidly replacing expatriate nurses in all the hospitals.

The incidence of disease throughout the country has been drastically reduced. No more so than amongst the very young, where an immunization programme was established throughout the Sultanate some years ago. There has been an interesting negative side effect of this. Formerly, because of the high infant mortality rate, Omanis were accustomed to having large families. Now that the mortality rate has been drastically reduced the tradition of large families has tended to continue. The Minister of Health told me of one man he knew who had twenty children. The size of a family is still a source of pride. The Sultan has publicly exhorted his people to limit their families to a maximum of five children: otherwise an employment problem exists for the future. The resources of the Sultanate will only support a limited population.

A good example of how disease is being stamped out amongst the population at large is the case of malaria. Malaria was rampant throughout all regions of Oman where there was cultivation. The anopheles mosquitoes bred in the stagnant pools of irrigation water in the date gardens. As I mentioned in an earlier chapter, when travelling in the Interior I always camped at night away from the areas of cultivation and never had malaria: nor did I take any anti-malaria precautions. The method of eradication of malaria is simple and effective. Each area of cultivation is divided into seven sub-divisions, and a local farmer is employed to spray all stagnant water in each sub-division once a week. Local inspectors are employed to supervise the spraying and know which sub-division should be sprayed on any particular day. If the local farmer is not doing his job he is sacked and another replaces him. By this method malaria was totally eradicated from the Sharqiya region over a period of two years. The same methods are being used on the Batinah Coast and other cultivated areas, and it is confidently expected that malaria will have been eradicated from the entire Sultanate by the end of the present century.

Some problems have arisen from the changed and improved living conditions over recent years. Reference has already been made to the youth explosion due to the drastic reduction of the infant mortality rate. At the other end of the scale life expectancy has been increased by modem medicine and this has resulted in an increase in the incidence of diabetes. Trachoma, the blinding infection caused by bad hygiene, which was so prevalent in the towns and villages of the Interior is still a problem.

APPENDIX III

Demand for Education

When I left the Sultanate in 1969 there were only three boys' schools of primary standard in Muscat, Muttrah and Salalah, and no girls' schools. In the larger centres of population there were Koranic schools, often consisting of classes held under the shade of trees where children were taught to read and write. Even so, illiteracy was widespread. I remember trying to teach one of my drivers the Arabic alphabet. Richer Omanis sent their children abroad illegally, usually to Kuwait, to be educated. Sayyis Tariq, a half-brother of the Sultan, actually went abroad with his family into voluntary exile in order to get his children educated.

It is not surprising, therefore, that on the accession of Sultan Qaboos bin Said in 1970 there was an urgent demand for education throughout the Sultanate. This was easier said than done owing to the complete lack of Omani teachers and premises for schools. However, progress was made at commendable speed with the recruitment of expatriate Arab teachers, mostly Egyptian and Jordanian. In fact in almost all schools for many years only the headteachers were Omanis. I remember being taken round a girls' school in Salalah in 1976 where the teachers were Sudanese women. There was also a school which I visited in Salalah where all the students were orphan boys who had been brainwashed by the communists and were being de-indoctrinated.

During the first year of development the demand for

education was so great that in many cases classes were held in tents and in shifts. Another point which must not be overlooked is that, great as the demand was for the education of children and the priority given to it, there was also a pressing demand by adults for education as well as the abolition of illiteracy.

The progress achieved in the 25 years between 1970 and 1995 is easily illustrated by the current state of education in the Sultanate, where a standard system of education through primary, intermediate and secondary schools to university and technical colleges is now in place. The guidance and inspiration for all this has come from Sultan Qaboos, and great credit is also due to Shaikh Amer bin Ali Omeir al Marhoobi, who started as assistant Head of the Department of Information. His particular contribution was the planning of the Sultan Qaboos University, which he saw through to its completion and became its first Vice Chancellor. Now retired, Shaikh Amer has played a major role in many aspects of the development of education in the Sultanate.

In accordance with Omani tradition schools are organized on a single sex basis. I visited a number of schools over the years throughout the Sultanate and the only exceptions I saw to this were in the rural areas of Dhofar where, due to lack of facilities at the time, children of both sexes were attending the same classes. At the Sultan Qaboos University students of both sexes attend the same lectures, but are seated separately.

Other aspects of education which had to be developed at the same time were teacher training, a national curriculum and the production of textbooks suitable for Omani education. A classic example of this was the case of history textbooks, where only books dealing with English history were originally available for schools as none of Omani history existed. In spite of the difficulties at the time all such problems were dealt with and overcome with remarkable speed. Teacher training colleges were established for male and female teachers with the result that by 1995 there were over 21,000 trained Omani teachers of both sexes in the 947 schools throughout the Sultanate; and using an Omani curriculum nearly 80 per cent of teachers are now Omani. Although the State system of education is predominant, private education has been encouraged, and in 1995 there were 69 private schools with 12,753 pupils and 881 teachers.

The abolition of illiteracy throughout the Sultanate is currently being given considerable importance as well as adult education, particularly for women, whose demands are considerable. The Ministry of Education gives special training to teachers who specialize in teaching illiterate adults as well as adult training. Currently there are 250 Literacy Centres throughout the country with more than 8,400 adult students, and 176 Adult Centres with 9,800 students.

Another problem that had to be confronted was the teaching of English, a knowledge of which was particularly important for students going on from school to university both at home and abroad. Science-based courses at the Sultan Qaboos University are conducted in English. Before 1970 when I was living and working in Oman, few Omanis could speak English and virtually none in the interior. Of necessity, therefore, when I was working in the interior I had to learn to speak Arabic, as spoken locally, from the basis I had already acquired. Now the situation is totally altered, as English is taught in all schools to a remarkably high standard; and it is only some of those of the older generation who have no knowledge of the language.

Considerable emphasis has been given to the education and training of the handicapped and disabled and a special Welfare Department of the Ministry of Social Affairs and Labour was set up in 1980 for this purpose. A major achievement in this area has been the Centre for the Care and Rehabilitation of the Disabled at al Khoodh, near Muscat, which was opened in 1987, and which I visited shortly after its opening, and impressed me greatly. Since then several centres, known as Wafa Centres, for the care and rehabilitation of disabled children have been opened in various regions of the Sultanate.